Golf Driving Techniques from Golfing

Golf Driving Techniques from Golfing Greats and Golf Stories

Proven Golf Driving Techniques from Dustin Johnson, Rory, Jason Day, Justin Thomas, Bubba Watson, and many more

Includes Exercises and Drills

Presented by The Team Golfwell

Published by: Pacific Trust Holdings NZ Ltd., 2017

Golf Driving Techniques from Golfing Greats and Golf Stories, Copyright © 2017, Pacific Trust Holdings NZ Ltd. All rights reserved. No part of this book may be reproduced or transmitted in any form or by any means, electronic or mechanical, including photocopying, recording or by any information storage and retrieval system, without written permission from the author, except for brief quotations as would be used in a review.

This book contains Exercises and Drills. You should always seek medical advice from your medical professional and/or check with your physician before doing the exercises and drills in this book or in any exercise program to avoid possible injury.

Golf Driving Techniques from Golfing Greats and Golf Stories

Praises received:

"I can hit it 10 -15 yards farther with less effort after reading this book. I stopped trying to kill the ball and learned it's not hard if you just let it fly. Enjoyable reading and loved the stories and exercises and drills for using the driver. It's good to know how the top PGA Tour pros do it all. Thank you."

    -R Davis, Kansas City

"This book is a great read and wish it was put out earlier. Great practical advice from the Pros. Liked learning how Justin Thomas hits it so far for his size. Ideas from the sport psychologists keep my head clear and balanced. I easily hit it farther after learning it's not hard to do from reading this book. Great job, Golfwell!

    -P Johnson, Las Vegas

"Driving is now my easiest shot. Very well done. I've read a lot of confusing stuff from others promising bigger drives but this one book is all I need."

    -M Miller, Miami

Golf Driving Techniques from Golfing Greats and Golf Stories

This book is dedicated to the late and great, Arnold Palmer, who we had the pleasure of meeting at the bar at Bay Hill GC.

"What other people may find in poetry or art museums, I find in the flight of a good drive."
- Arnold Palmer

Golf Driving Techniques from Golfing Greats and Golf Stories

-Photo courtesy of Jeff Farsai, Long Beach, CA

Golf Driving Techniques from Golfing Greats and Golf Stories

Contents

INTRODUCTION: 15

1. "TEE IT HIGH AND LET IT FLY!" - Increase your "Angle of attack" like Justin Thomas 16

2. "HERE ARE SOME SIMPLE ADJUSTMENTS TO HIT IT EVEN LONGER" says Dustin Johnson 22

3. "YOU DON'T HAVE TO BE A BIG GUY" says Rickie Fowler 24

4. "DON'T THINK ABOUT WHERE THE BALL WILL GO," says Ben Hogan 26

5. "A SIX IRON SHOT GOING 1,000,000+ MILES?"...............29

6. TIGER "JUMPS" AT THE INSTANT OF CONTACT (BOTH FEET MOMENTARILY COME OFF THE GROUND) 31

7. IN A LONG SLUMP WITH YOUR DRIVING THE BALL? "TAKE A BREAK," says Jim McLean 33

8. "GET A DRIVER WITH MORE LOFT," says Bubba Watson 35

9. GETTING "OVER THE HILL?" USE WEIGHTED CLUBS TO MAINTAIN YOUR DRIVING STRENGTH like Vijay. 37

10. ANOTHER SO CALLED "OVER THE HILL" GUY HITTING IT BIG is Jeff Sluman 38

11. BOMBTECH'S 460 CC GRENADE DRIVER. 39

12. "TAKE THE DRIVER AWAY WIDE" says Tiger 40

13. "SWING WITH GOOD TEMPO" says Rory.................42

14. "YOU CAN HIT IT VERY FAR WITH A SHORT BACKSWING," says J. B. Holmes 44

15. "STRANGE PLACES TO FIND A GOLF BALL." 45

16. "GRIP IT AND RIP IT" says John Daly...............................49

17. THE 2016 LONG DRIVE CHAMP - 149 MPH SWING SPPED. 51

18. DAVIS LOVE III SAYS, "I'M 53 YEARS OLD AND HIT IT FURTHER NOW."....................53

19. GARY WOODLAND'S THOUGHTS ON HOW TO HIT IT LONG. 55

20. "SWING FROM THE GROUND UP," says Greg Norman...................................57

21. "THE LONGEST GOLF DRIVE ON EARTH."...............59

22. "HOW DO I COMPARE WITH THE AVERAGE GOLFER IN DRIVING DISTANCE?" HERE'S THE STATICSTICS..61

23. "HERE'S HOW TO PICK UP 10-20 YARDS ON YOUR DRIVE," says Robert Garrigus. 63

24. HOW MIKE WEIR AND PHIL DRIVE UNDER PRESSURE 65

25. JACK NICKLAUS SAYS TO "MANAGE YOUR DRIVES." ...69

26. "YOU NEED TO CATCH IT ON THE UPSWING IF YOU WANT DISTANCE," says Justin Rose 71

27. HERE'S TIPS FOR AMATUERS ON YOUR DRIVING," says Jason Day. 74

28. "RELY ON MAKING A GOOD TURN WITH YOUR SHOULDERS," says Fred Couples. 77

29. "SEVEN SIMPLE WAYS TO GET YOUR BLOOD MOVING TO YOUR MUSCLES AND HIT IT LONGER" 79

30. "BASIC STEPS IN DRIVING AND HOW TO GET YOUR GAME BACK" says Jordan Spieth 82

31. LOUIS OOSTHOUSEN 500 YARD DRIVE..........................85

32. "PRACTICE HARD AND SOMETIMES YOU GET LUCKY," says Andrew McGee 86

33. LONG DISTANCE AND ACCURACY? How to do it Sergio's way. 88

34. FRANCESCO MOLINARI SAYS, "CHOOSE A SMALL TARGET." 91

35. "YOUR DRIVER MAY BE STRAIGHTER THAN YOUR THREE WOOD UNDER THE LAWS OF PHYSICS FOR AMATEUR GOLFERS." 93

36. "TEE THE BALL MY WAY," says Billy Horschel 96

37. BROOKS KOEPKA TIPS FOR A BIG DRIVE WHEN YOU NEED ONE. 98

38. "TO HIT IT BIG, SET UP CORRECTLY," says Adam Scott 100

39. "BIG DRIVING IS NOT WHAT YOU REALLY WANT," says Larry Mize. 102

40. "I JUST EXECUTE BASIC TECHNIQUES FOR A LONG DRIVE," says Tony Finau 103

41. "WHAT MEN CAN LEARN FROM LADIES LONG DRIVING - WITH AN AVERAGE SWING SPEED OF 95 MPH." 106

42. "TWO THINGS TO CURE A SLICE" 109

44. "SOME SIMPLE POINTS TO REMEMBER" 114

45. "JEFF BARDEL DRIVES IT 288 YARDS WITH ONLY ONE ARM." 116

46. GET BACK TO BASICS. 120

"Focus on Remedies, not on faults"

-Jack Nicklaus

Golf Driving Techniques from Golfing Greats and Golf Stories

INTRODUCTION:

There's a lot of complicated advice around on how to drive a longer ball from many fine people - but many of these fine people haven't won any Major Golf Tournaments like the golfers featured in this book.

Reading about how to hit it longer is very helpful but keep in mind your local PGA teaching professional is usually the best source, since you're getting a professional opinion on a pro watching your individual swing technique.

But, if you want to know how the best in golf hit it far, this book is an excellent reference of the techniques, and equipment used by the best players in golf.

There's nothing too complicated in this book to help you drive the ball longer. We try to keep the techniques presented simple to make it easier for you to make small changes to allow you to hit it longer off the tee. You will get results. Enjoy!

1. "TEE IT HIGH AND LET IT FLY!" - Increase your "Angle of attack" like Justin Thomas

Justin Thomas is 5 feet 10 inches tall, weighs 145 lbs. and uses a 917D3 driver (Titleist) with a 9.5-degree loft.

He averages 306.7 yards in driving distance on the tour.

"I hit the ball with a high angle of attack," says Justin. "You've got to catch the ball on your upswing."

See his swing here >
https://www.youtube.com/watch?v=IDtQ4UT7yA0&feature=youtu.be

The long version of his swing is here >
https://youtu.be/fovTw4WU28c

He basically does two things:

1. Justin hits the ball in the center of the driver face. He's consistent doing this. Also, he keeps his head still and behind the ball.

2. He impacts the ball on the beginning of his upswing. Justin's angle of attack is between 4 and 5 degrees upward.

Justin recommends, "Keep a good firm base in the ground." He adds, "Keep the inside of your right heel and foot stable and firmly on the ground."

"When I feel I have a good firm base on the ground, I can use my legs to the best of my ability to hit up on the ball."

DRILL: SIMPLE STEPS TO INCREASE YOUR ANGLE OF ATTACK

1. Angle of Attack: "Do a slow practice swing and find your position 2." (Note: "Pos. 2 is the lowest point of the arc where your clubhead is closest to the ground.")

"The following picture shows 3 positions as the club descends on the downswing."

"The first position is position 1, then 2, then the last position is position 3."

2. Tee the ball forward to position 3 this will increase your angle of attack:

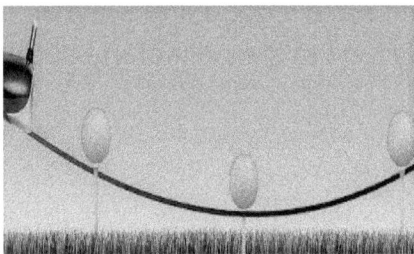

3. Lower your right shoulder so your right hand can easily reach the top of your right knee.

4. The handle of the driver should be pointing at your midsection.

5. Swing at your normal swing speed.

Keep practicing to embed this in your game.

A True Story

A Narrative from a Former High Handicapper

"I was a high handicapper and read about increasing the angle of attack."

"The first time I tried teeing the ball forward a few inches happened on the first tee of a Charity 4-man scramble tournament."

"My other three friends had handicaps of 2, 14 and 17."

"My driving distance generally is in the range of 200 – 205-yards."

"The scramble rules required each player's drive to be used at least three times and each player had to use a shot of each of the 4 par three holes (which was a worry since I was the shortest hitter)."

"I was third to hit off the first tee."

"I teed the ball up higher and placed my tee and ball a few inches in front of my normal tee position. The ball looked odd to me. It was teed too far forward. I relaxed and made a smooth swing at normal speed."

"Whack!"

I was amazed to watch my ball grow smaller in the distance then bouncing high on the fairway and stopping about 235 yards down just past the first two drives hit by the 14 and 17 handicappers."

"The other three in the group expressed simple comments to me, like "Nice drive" "You caught that one" etc. I was nonchalant hiding my enthusiasm over this simple technique. But I wasn't convinced yet if this really worked."

"After several holes, three of my drives were already used."

"*Amazing,* I thought, but I didn't say anything about it. I kept on hitting it longer with less effort."

"As the day went on, my confidence grew and carried over to my making better shots and putts."

"We didn't win the tournament, but placed in the prizes."

"To maintain this technique, I reflect on this first time I used an increased angle of attack and relax."

"It is probably the best zone and best focus I've ever been in. I know I'm playing well."

"It doesn't happen very often in golf, and it's really fun to happen."

"It's probably maybe only the second time it's ever happened to me."

    -Justin Thomas

2. "HERE ARE SOME SIMPLE ADJUSTMENTS TO HIT IT EVEN LONGER" says Dustin Johnson

Dustin Johnson is 6 feet 4 inches tall, 190 lbs. and uses a 10.5 degree Taylor Made M1 460 Driver.

Like Justin Thomas, D.J. recommends teeing the ball up higher. D.J then widens his stance and drops his right shoulder to hit the ball on the upswing.

Dustin recommends keeping both legs flexed during the swing. "I turn my hips first as I begin my downswing pushing with my right leg muscles," says D.J. He recommends keeping the swing smooth and avoid over swinging.

"Let the driver come down …. It's accelerating on the downswing and simply allow it to happen."

"It's best to keep an even tempo at a speed you feel most comfortable and confident."

Golf Driving Techniques from Golfing Greats and Golf Stories

DJ says, "Don't force it fast from the top of the downswing. It's much better to be smooth and let the club accelerate."

He explains an easy way to determine if you are accelerating is, "To have the club whip around to a high finish after hitting the drive."

"I try to play the game like a gentleman and be respectful to all. That's how the game should be played."

-Dustin Johnson

3. "YOU DON'T HAVE TO BE A BIG GUY" says Rickie Fowler

Rickie Fowler is 5 feet 9 inches tall and weighs 150 lbs. His drives average 290+ yards. He uses a 9-degree Cobra King Ltd. Driver.

Rickie says, "Tee the ball higher and tee it even with your left little toe when you need a long drive."

"Maintain your head behind the ball and drop your right shoulder too when you set up," says Rickie. He takes a wide stance with his weight evenly balanced.

"Let the club do the work and stay relaxed." says Rickie, "Just stay loose and let it go."

DRILL:

Tee the ball even with your left little toe and a bit higher and drop your right shoulder. Maintain your head position behind the ball.

Golf Driving Techniques from Golfing Greats and Golf Stories

"My grandpa was the one; he started taking me to the range when I was about two and introduced me to the game…. I have an eye for seeing things differently. Somehow, I just see shots in my head."

"That was really all he (Grandpa) had to do was let me hit a golf ball and kind of fell in love with it from there…."

    -Rickie Fowler

4. "DON'T THINK ABOUT WHERE THE BALL WILL GO," says Ben Hogan

Years ago, a PGA Tour player asked Ben Hogan how to hit his drives further.

Hogan simply told him, "Go to the range after every golf round and hit balls with his driver swinging as fast as he could but not to swing so fast so that you lose your balance."

"Don't worry about where the ball goes, just work on building up your speed" said Hogan.

"Repeating a fast swing (up to the point of losing your balance) after every round trains your coordination and helps you learn to swing faster," said Hogan.

Hogan also pointed out, "It's very easy to lose your balance when you swing fast and losing your balance will, of course, cost you distance."

DRILL:

A very simple drill: After a round, hit balls for 10 minutes building up your speed and swinging as fast as you can (but not too fast where you begin to lose balance).

"People have always been telling me what I can't do. I guess I have wanted to show them. That's been one of my driving forces all my life."

    -Ben Hogan

Not worrying is very important on the golf course according to Dr. Bob Rotella, the renowned Golf sport psychologist.

"Staying in the present is a simple concept but one of the most difficult to put into practice."

"When you worry about what the other players are doing, or if you want to hit a good drive, you are actually thinking about a future event."

"Worrying about what others are doing is actually thinking about the final result which is a future event."

"Whether you are going to hit a good drive or not is also thinking about a future event."

"Do not dwell in the past."

"Do not dream of the future."

"Concentrate the mind on the present moment."

    -Buddha

5. "A SIX IRON SHOT GOING 1,000,000+ MILES?"

Have you ever wondered who hit the longest golf shot in history? It wasn't with a driver.

Michael Lopez-Alegria is a Spanish American astronaut born in 1958. He has degrees in Systems Engineering, and Aeronautical Engineering. He speaks English, Spanish, French and Russian fluently. He spent 6 months on a space station.

Lopez said, "During a spacewalk, I hit a golf ball with a six iron and the ball traveled more than 1,000,000 miles before disintegrating into the earth's atmosphere."

Golf Driving Techniques from Golfing Greats and Golf Stories

6. TIGER "JUMPS" AT THE INSTANT OF CONTACT (BOTH FEET MOMENTARILY COME OFF THE GROUND)

Most of us have heard the expression, "You came out of your shoes when you hit that one."

In his heyday, if Tiger didn't have his shoe laces tied, he might have just done that many times.

He slightly comes off the ground at the instant of contact. "You can see him do it in slow motion > https://www.youtube.com/watch?v=Ur9W47rjF80

His entire body lifts up off the ground for a fraction of a second. Rickie Fowler does this too.

Golf Driving Techniques from Golfing Greats and Golf Stories

"People don't understand that when I grew up, I wasn't the most talented, or the biggest, fastest or strongest. I had a very strong work ethic, and that's what made me."

-Tiger Woods

7. IN A LONG SLUMP WITH YOUR DRIVING THE BALL? "TAKE A BREAK," says Jim McLean

If you're in a golf slump and have been that way for a while, Jim McLean recommends you take a break and do *anything* but golf for a while.

McLean talks about the great "Slammin Sammy" Snead. Sam won more golf tournaments than anyone during his career. Sam would go into slumps and just gave it up for weeks and did other things. After a few weeks, Sam returned and began winning again.

Hal Sutton nearly lost his card. Hal gave up golf and met with Jackie Burke. Hal went to Jackie, since "Jackie coached top players and had a feel for the mental game and the importance of confidence."

Jackie helped Hal by complimenting him making Hal realize he actually had a lot of talent. Hal started to understand himself and believe in his own ability.

Hal came back on the tour and started winning more tournaments.

Simple things like compliments and emphasizing your past accomplishments fosters confidence. Your muscles react better when you are confident vs. your muscles tightening up when you lack confidence. Tom Brady agrees:

"When I'm out on the football field, I have so much confidence in what I'm doing… those blessed with confidence are the most competitive and have the biggest heart."

-Tom Brady

8. "GET A DRIVER WITH MORE LOFT," says Bubba Watson

Bubba Watson is 6 feet 3 inches, weighs 180 lbs. and generates a lot of swing speed (126 mph). He uses a Ping G25 Driver with an 8.5-degree loft with a 44.5" shaft.

There are several simple things you can do according to Bubba to hit it longer.

Bubba understands most average golfers are physically unable to generate the amount of clubhead speed he does. So, he recommends three things:

1. Get your equipment checked out on present technology. "Does your driver have the right loft and shaft best suited to you? The right loft and shaft type will maximize your distance," says Bubba, and, "Radar devices (found in most golf shops) will quickly help determine the best suited loft and shaft for your swing."

2. "Take a wide stance," says Bubba. "I take a wide stance when I need a long drive."

Golf Driving Techniques from Golfing Greats and Golf Stories

Bubba also angles his right foot out 45 degrees so it's easier to clear his hips (Bubba is a southpaw so his lead foot is his right foot which he angles out 45 degrees). He says, "I got this from watching Tiger turn his lead foot out 45 degrees," and, "I tried it myself and it works when you take a wide stance."

3. "A long shaft isn't the answer either," says Bubba. "You'll hit the sweet spot more if you use a shorter shaft." Most stores have drivers with 45 ½ inch shafts. Bubbas uses a 44 and ½ inch shaft.

"The shorter the shaft, the easier it is," says Bubba. "If you hit it on the sweet spot, you'll get much more distance without extra effort."

9. GETTING "OVER THE HILL?" USE WEIGHTED CLUBS TO MAINTAIN YOUR DRIVING STRENGTH like Vijay.

Stay in shape like Vijay Singh does. Vijay is 6 feet 2 inches tall, and weighs 208 lbs. He's 53 years old. He uses a 9 degree TaylorMade M1 driver.

Vijay practices his swing using weighted clubs. At 53, Vijay says, "I still can hit it as far as I could ever."

Slotted weights work better than trying to swing holding two or three clubs at a time. Slotted weights are available in shops and online.

10. ANOTHER SO CALLED "OVER THE HILL" GUY HITTING IT BIG is Jeff Sluman

Jeff Sluman ranks in the top 10 in driving distance on the Champions Tour averaging about 301 yards.

Jeff is 5 feet 7 inches tall, weighs 140 lbs., is 59 years old, and uses a TaylorMade R11S Driver.

Jeff says, "I play the ball forward and catch it cleanly on the upswing."

Jeff has almost a 5-degree angle of attack. Very similar to Justin Thomas. It's simply striking the ball with an ascending hit.

"And, the more you widen your stance and the more you are getting your head behind the ball. This makes it easier to increase your angle of attack," says Jeff.

11. BOMBTECH'S 460 CC GRENADE DRIVER.

Have you ever heard of Bombtech Golf?

Bombtech is golf club manufacturing company which has come out with a driver (they refer to it as their Grenade driver). They sell these for $299 at the time of this writing.

The club isn't available in retail stores yet. You can buy it from Bombtech, the manufacturer. It's relatively new.

The reviews on this driver are fairly good so far.

The well-known golf blog "The Sand Trap" has independent reviews and comments about this Bombtech Driver. Search for Bombtech in the blog and you'll see several reviews.

12. "TAKE THE DRIVER AWAY WIDE" says Tiger

Tiger Woods is 6 feet 1 inch tall, weighs 185 lbs. and used a Nike driver. Since Nike has gotten out of the golf equipment business Tiger has been using a Taylor Made M2 460 Driver with a 10.5-degree loft.

"I don't use a long shaft since I'm more concerned in increasing the percentages to hit the ball on the sweet spot."

Tiger recommends taking the driver away with a wide arc. "Don't slash quickly at the ball which I see a lot of amateurs do when they want more speed," Tiger says.

"If your diver is longer than 43.5 inches, try choking down. You'll hit the center of your driver more," says Tiger.

For many years, Tiger has and still uses a driver with a shaft of 43.5.

"Well, you know, a lot of people look at the negative things, the things that they did wrong. I like to think about the things I did right. I like to stress on things from a positive standpoint for great reinforcement."

-Tiger Woods

13. "SWING WITH GOOD TEMPO" says Rory

Rory McIroy is 5 feet 10 inches, weighs 161 lbs. He hits a Callaway Great Big Bertha Epic Sub Zero with 9 degrees of loft. He averages over 300 yards.

Rory has said many times, "I know I have the ability to hit it very far if I need a long drive, but if a long drive isn't needed, I prefer to keep the ball in the fairway."

"I practice listening to music," says Rory. "Good tempo results in good solid strikes." Rory listens to music like Coldplay tunes.

"Once you're loosened up and confident and swinging with a comfortable balance, forget about swinging as fast or as hard as you can," says Rory. "Just think about swinging with good tempo."

Rory averages a swing speed around 119 mph.

A simple relaxed tempo helps Rory turn his hips. "I begin my downswing by turning my left knee and hips just a fraction of a second before bringing the club down. This motion give you distance."

Rory's dad tells a story, "Rory was able to drive the ball 40 yards off the tee by the time he was just two years old."

Rory's Dad says, "Rory was shooting level par at his home course at the age of 11."

He starts to turn his left knee and hips a fraction of a second before beginning his downswing>
https://www.youtube.com/watch?v=fb6mBZ3Kb_Q

DRILL:

You can improve your balance and tempo:

1. Take your normal stance but keep your feet together. Do 20 half swings back and forth slowly and smoothly with a wedge.

You should try to keep a comfortable balance. If you start to lose balance do your half swings slower.

14. "YOU CAN HIT IT VERY FAR WITH A SHORT BACKSWING," says J. B. Holmes

J.B. Holmes has won the Tour's Driving Distance category twice. Over his career, J.B. usually ranks among the top 7 in driving distance. J.B. has an abbreviated golf swing.

He's 5 feet 11 inches, weighs 190 lbs. and hits a TaylorMade M1 430 Driver with a 9.5-degree loft.

Holmes takes a wide shoulder turn and coils. "I begin my downswing with a strong sharp turn of my hips followed by pulling his arms downward."

J. B. pauses at the top, then takes a short (3/4) backswing. "I press down with my left heel, and my hips turn, and then my shoulders and arms uncoil," says J.B. His swing speed averages 125.2 mph.

"It's simple. The more I pull my arms down, the faster the club head follows," says J.B.

15. "STRANGE PLACES TO FIND A GOLF BALL."

Driving a ball may lead you into the woods. Jimmy Demaret said, you'll find a lot of big hitters searching for their ball in the woods."

Cactus: If you strike a cactus with your golf ball they usually embed into the cactus.

Killer swans will attack you if they have signets near.

"A swan will attack you by repeatedly hitting you with the large (carpal) bone in their wings which will bruise or break your arm," say golf course maintenance people.

Seagulls will pick up your ball and fly it away. Dogs will pick up your ball too. Under Rule 18-1, you can replace your ball.

Crappers and Outhouses: ?! Golf course maintenance people say, "There's lots of balls at the bottom of the long drops. While doing their business, people check their golf balls for nicks and drop them."

It's not the best place to use a ball retriever.

True Story

"I was looking for a ball just off the fairway in Queensland, Australia, and stepped into a funnel web spider's nest." A funnel web spider is one of the most venomous spiders known – the picture below is the female.

"I was told the male funnel web can get as big as your hand. It's hairy with fangs - a very scary spider."

"Luckily, a guy in our foursome told me, 'I'd forget about finding your ball, mate,' so I got out of there."

Golf Driving Techniques from Golfing Greats and Golf Stories

*

Florida golf courses have alligators.

The Port Labelle Inn & Oxbow Golf Club, near the Everglades, has signs posted on the course,

>"Do Not Molest the Alligators."

We may be wrong, but we don't think many golfers would jump on the back of a gator and start to tease it?

"The only time I ever took out a one-iron was to kill a tarantula."

"And it took a seven to do that."

    -Jim Murray

16. "GRIP IT AND RIP IT" says John Daly

"His driving is unbelievable."

"I don't go that far on my holidays."

-Ian Baker-Finch, on John Daly

John Daly is 5 foot 11 inches and weighs around 240 lbs. He uses a TaylorMade M1430 Driver with 9.50-degree loft. He's probably the most well-known long hitter.

In the 1990s, John Daly gave a lot of inspiration to golfers all over the world with his amazing long backswing which features his unique way of extremely hinging his wrists way back so the shaft is far past parallel to the ground.

Where J.B. Holmes' swing is abbreviated, John Daly's swing is exaggerated.

Golf Driving Techniques from Golfing Greats and Golf Stories

John says, "I do a 90 degree turn with the shoulders and transfer my weight from my right side on the upswing and to the left side on the downswing."

"My hips turn 45 degrees away from the ball and then back again. But the power comes from unhinging my wrists."

In 1997, John was the first PGA Tour player to average more than 300 yards in driving distance.

John keeps a positive outlook. "Life is nothing but a memory."

"People who dwell on the bad ones aren't going to have a whole lot of good ones coming up," says John.

"I taught myself how to swing for power and distance."

In 2009, John's swing speed was 121.49 miles per hour. John's golf ball speed coming off his driver is 179.32 mph.

He's a good example of doing whatever works.

Golf Driving Techniques from Golfing Greats and Golf Stories

17. THE 2016 LONG DRIVE CHAMP - 149 MPH SWING SPPED.

He's 29, 6 foot 4 inches tall and weighs 270 lbs. His driver: a Callaway XR 16 LDA with a five-degree loft.

His name is Joe Miller and he won the 2016 event.

Joe says, "I clear my hips early and this creates the proper angle for the club coming into the ball."

"When I turn my left hip out, my right elbow snaps in right away after clearing my left hip," Joe adds.

"By quickly turning my left hip at the top of the swing, I snap my right elbow into my body which creates a whipping motion."

Joe's swing speed is over 140 mph.

Joe is a student of the great Ben Hogan. "Ben told golfers to pretend there is an elastic cord tied to their left hip which snaps the hip back at the top of the swing."

Joe says, "If I start hitting to the left side, I know I'm not clearing my hips as fast as I should since my upper body is coming around too quick before my left hip clears.

His winning drive is here > https://www.youtube.com/watch?v=R01eLwZnByg

Hitting the ball in the center of the driver, of course, makes a big difference in length:

"If you're struggling to hit the ball solid…make half swings where your left arm gets no higher than parallel to the ground on the backswing."

"And your right arm gets no higher than parallel on the follow-through."

"When you start consistently making center-face contact, …go back to the full motion."

    -David Leadbetter

18. DAVIS LOVE III SAYS, "I'M 53 YEARS OLD AND HIT IT FURTHER NOW."

Davis Love III is 53 years old, 6 foot 3 inches, weighs 175 lbs., and hits a TaylorMade SLDR driver with a 9-degree loft.

Love averages 302.9 yards off the tee. Ten years ago, he averaged 290.8 off the tee.

"My father taught me to use my left arm as the lead arm in my swing," says Davis. "He taught me to use my left arm had me hitting balls only with my left arm."

"Then he had me lightly place my right hand on my left hand and had me continue to hit balls with my left arm."

"My right hand wouldn't grip the club - it would only rest over my left hand."

"And, I hit ball after ball at every practice doing this," said Davis.

Davis works on his takeaway. "I have a tendency to pick my club up on takeaway rather than drawing it back on a wide," says Davis. "I learned to concentrate on bringing the club back slowly and as wide as I can."

"This stops me from picking the club up and bringing it sharply down which causes me to hit it left," says Davis.

"I saw the club head at the top of Love's golf swing and you could almost do chin-ups on it."

-Anon.

19. GARY WOODLAND'S THOUGHTS ON HOW TO HIT IT LONG.

Gary Woodland is 6 feet 1 inch, weighs 195 lbs. and uses a 9.5 degree TaylorMade M2. He averages 304.2 yards driving.

In simple terms, Gary recommends four things:

1. "Take a wide stance, since a narrow stance will more likely than not make you lose your balance."

2. Gary does a very slow take away with his driver. He does this because he is the type of golfer that speeds his swing up at the end when he takes a slow deliberate start.

3. He starts his downswing as smooth as possible. "Many weekend golfers swing too hard at the ball from the top of their swing." Gary believes it's better to relax and concentrate on a smooth transition from the top of the swing to starting it downward to strike the ball.

4. "My goal is to hit the ball with the sweet spot of the face of the driver." To do this, Gary slows his swing down. "It's like baseball – swing like you are trying to hit a nice line drive rather than a home run into the upper deck."

Gary says, "A long drive will happen naturally and you don't force it in any way."

Gary recommends relaxation and concentration as Arnie has said many times, "Golf requires complete relaxation and complete concentration," and he added, "The secret of concentration is the secret of self-discovery. Reach inside yourself. Find your own resources and select the ones you need to meet the challenge."

20. "SWING FROM THE GROUND UP," says Greg Norman

Greg Norman is 62 years old and 6 feet tall, and was #1 golfer in the world for 331 weeks.

His drives averaged 293 yards. He used a Cobra persimmon wood driver.

He has one simple tip for average golfers. "Some average golfers swing from the top without any leg motion."

"The proper way to hit it is to bend your knees and sweep your arms hitting the ball on your upswing."

Greg encourages amateurs to watch present-day tour players drive the ball. "They stay behind the ball and their entire body lifts very slightly up as the club impacts the golf ball," says Greg.

According to Greg, "If you can get into a coordinated sweeping motion lifting your body up when striking the ball, while keeping your head still and behind the ball, the average golfer would hit the drive 20 yards further."

Jack Nicklaus was a major influence to Greg Norman and he learned the game by reading Jack's book, "Golf My Way."

"I never hit a shot, even in practice, without having a very sharp picture of it in my head. It's like watching a color movie."

"First, I 'see' the ball in a position where I want it to finish, nice and high and sitting up high on the bright green grass."

"Then the scene flips and I 'see' the ball going there: its path, trajectory, and shape, even its behavior on landing."

    -Jack Nicklaus

21. "THE LONGEST GOLF DRIVE ON EARTH."

It's 1972. Mike Austin is going to hit a drive at the U.S. National Seniors Open in Las Vegas. He's on the par 4, 455 yard, 5th hole.

The Golf course in Las Vegas has an elevation of a couple of thousand feet.

At the time Mike hit the drive, he said, "There was a strong tailwind."

"My drive flies over 400 yards in the air and hits the fairway but continues bouncing through the green and finally stops 60 yards past the flag," said Mike.

"To this day, this 515-yard drive is the longest recorded tournament drive according to PGA Records."

It's also listed as the longest tournament drive in the Guinness Book of Records.

Mike, a big guy at 6' 2" said, feet two inches, and added, "It was like God hit it. Who can hit a ball that far? No one. I feel like I got some assistance from God."

Mike says, "Good arm extension will help you hit it long."

Mike lived to the age of 95 and passed in 2005.

Keep a clear head to hit it long, and relax the nerves.

"Nerves will make your backswing short. If you're on the first tee, have a single thought of making a nice rhythmic shoulder turn…and, take your time, the ball isn't going anywhere."

-Butch Harmon

22. "HOW DO I COMPARE WITH THE AVERAGE GOLFER IN DRIVING DISTANCE?" HERE'S THE STATICSTICS.

Game Golf collects statistics on the driving distance of average golfers.

Statistics collected by Game Golf:

"Golfers with handicaps less than five drive an average distance of 250 yards."

"Golfers with handicaps from 5 to 19 average from 225 to 240 yards."

"Golfers with handicaps from 20 to 28 average from 190 to 215 yards."

"Golfers with handicaps over 28 average around 180 yards."

"Driving distances for age groups from 20 to 40 range from 230 to 240."

"Driving distances for age groups from 40 to 60 range from 210 to 230."

"Driving distances for age groups over 60 range from 190 to 210."

A tip from Sean Foley:

"The secret is in the squat. Let your knees flare out as you start down, and you'll pick up some noticeable distance."

-Sean Foley, Coach of Justin Rose

23. "HERE'S HOW TO PICK UP 10-20 YARDS ON YOUR DRIVE," says Robert Garrigus.

Robert Garrigus is 5' 11" tall, weighs 175 lbs., is 39 years old. He hits a TaylorMade M1 460 with a 9.5-degree loft.

Robert first recommends, "Get your equipment checked out to make sure you are using the right clubs, shaft, etc. for your swing."

"But, an easier way to get 10 to 20 yards more on your drives is to establish a smooth rhythm beginning with your takeaway," says Robert.

He recommends, "Swing with only 90% of your power - even though that sounds just like the opposite of what you should do."

"Using less power actually results in more distance." Robert goes on to say, "Start each swing, 'Slow and low,'"

Robert has his caddie say, "Slow and low" to him at pressure times when he steps up to drive the ball.

"You'll get better contact going 'Slow and low' and you'll get more distance."

24. HOW MIKE WEIR AND PHIL DRIVE UNDER PRESSURE

"You just don't have the time to worry about what others are doing. You just want to take care of your own business."

"You are focused on that tee shot on the 18th tee and making it to the finish line."

"It's one of the most stressful moments in professional golf, but you have worked so hard to get to that point, that it really is fun."

-Mike Weir, 2003 Masters Champion

Mike Weir and Phil Mickleson are both left handed golfers, as you already know.

Mike is 5 feet 9 inches tall and weighs 155 lbs. and uses a TaylorMade M1 driver with a 9.5-degree loft.

"The average golfer doesn't generate the swing speed the professionals can, so it's best to concentrate on getting good contact."

Mike adds, "If your swing speed is 95 mph and you hit it in the middle of your driver, it will go further than trying to swing faster and hitting on the toe -- which you can easily do when you try to move your arms faster." And, Mike says, "That leads to inconsistency."

Instead, Mike suggests concentrating on tempo, make a full shoulder turn away from the ball and stay balanced. These fundamentals lead to longer distances.

Phil Mickleson is 6 feet 3 inches, 200 lbs. and uses a Callaway XR 16 Pro Sub Zero 8.5-degree driver.

Pressure?

Phil says, "Imagine it's Sunday, the final round, and I need a good drive to finish the last hole?"

"Here are some of my thoughts when teeing up the ball under pressure."

Phil went on to explain these ideas:

1. "When you have to get the ball in play, don't let negative thoughts enter your mind about what you *don't* want the ball to do." Phil says. He goes on to add, "If you do, you may wind up doing exactly that."

"You have to control your thoughts and stay in the present by picking your target and focusing on your target – take a positive approach," says Phil.

2. "Keep a swing thought of extending your arms all the way through the shot after striking the ball," says Phil.

Phil adds, "While your extending your arms, you are at the same time slightly coming up from the ground." (As Greg Norman recommended).

Phil says, "If you hit right handed, let your right leg slightly stand up rather than slide. That's the easiest way to come up from the ground."

3. Finally, Phil says to "Swing through the ball and as you come through the shot, keeping both arms extended as you strike the ball."

"I love competing against the best players. I have a huge challenge, and that's to win a U.S. Open and complete the Grand Slam. I enjoy that challenge."

"Every year it comes around, I get excited to try to conquer that opportunity. I love it."

      -Phil Mickelson

25. JACK NICKLAUS SAYS TO "MANAGE YOUR DRIVES."

Jack Nicklaus was one of the best, if not the best, golf course manager to ever play the game. He uses a twostep process:

1. Pick the target on the fairway vs. just hitting it into a fairway.

2. Decide on the shot that is going to get you there.

Jack says, "For example, the 18th hole at Muirfield Village has a creek going down the left side and bunkers on the right side." Jack then explains how to handle this.

"First consider the side you don't want to err on when you hit it off the tee." Jack explains, "It's better to err to the side of the bunkers on the right side, since driving the ball into the creek is a one stroke penalty."

"So, I decide to play the hole with a fading drive and starting it out down the left side of the fairway."

If he fades it too much, he'll be in the bunker rather than the creek and possibly save a stroke.

Jack also recommends, "When you decide you don't need to hit a driver on a par 4, you should hit your three-wood using a full swing rather than letting up on a driver."

"This is because, letting up on swinging a driver usually results in a poor shot when a normal swing with a three wood will get you where you want to be," says Jack.

"Ask yourself how many shots you would have saved if you always developed a strategy before you hit, always played within your capabilities, never lost you temper, and never got down on yourself."

-Jack Nicklaus

26. "YOU NEED TO CATCH IT ON THE UPSWING IF YOU WANT DISTANCE," says Justin Rose

Justin Rose is 6'2" 180 lbs. 36 years old and hits a 8.5 degree TaylorMade M2 driver.

Justin Rose says, "In order to get distance on your drive, you first need to tee the ball forward and tee it higher to catch the ball on your upswing."

"You begin your swing taking the club head away from the ball and loading your weight on your right side as if you were doing a squat to flex your glutes."

He explains, "Don't hurry your swing to get to the top of it."

"Think of it as loading up your swing with your right toe putting pressure to the ground."

"On the downswing, maintain your height, keeping pressure on the ground with his feet."

Halfway down on his downswing, he pushes the ground with his feet releasing the power he's built up in the swing.

DRILL:

Justin Rose explains this drill: "First drop your left foot back and put 90 percent of your weight on your right side."

"Then bring your arms to the top of your swing, but only practice swinging halfway down keeping your weight on your right side."

Justin concluded by saying, "If you keep repeating this motion you will recognize the balance and the power, your building up to drive the ball."

After winning the 2013 US Open:

"The thing I was most proud of about today's round was that on this course everybody is going to make mistakes, but sometimes it's hard to forget about it and let it go."

"After I made a double on 1, I was able to be patient and let it go and came back with birdies on 3 and 5."

"When I bogeyed 6, I was able to let it go and come back with a birdie on 8."

"I let go of some bad shots and forgot about it and moved on."

-Justin Rose

27. HERE'S TIPS FOR AMATUERS ON YOUR DRIVING," says Jason Day.

Jason Day is 6 feet and weighs 195 lbs. and now uses a TaylorMade M1 2017 with a 10.5-degree loft.

He has a wide takeaway with a straight left arm extending throughout his swing.> https://www.youtube.com/watch?v=e9bl20l882g.

Jason recommends amateurs to, "Make sure you tee the ball up aligned with the center of your driver."

Jason adds that amateurs don't always do this, "If you line it up with the toe or heel it will increase your chances for mishitting the drive."

"Be aware you don't want to sway away from the ball when you bring your club back on the upswing."

Jason adds, "Remember to turn instead of swaying off the ball when you bring the driver back."

Jason recommends, to practice swinging with an alignment stick instead of a weighted club.

"If you practice your swing using a light alignment stick you will be sensing how to swing faster."

He likes the alignment stick method. "Swinging two clubs or a weighted club will make you swing slower. You should learn how to swing fast and keep your balance."

"Swing wide on your take away keeping your hands as far away from you as you can," says Jason.

"Think about having high hands and keep both of your arms *straight on your downswing*." (emphasis added).

"My dad was the way he was, but he also gave me a motto: Never say die. Just to keep pushing and pushing, fighting until the end."

"He put it in my head that you're always going to fight, and you're always going to beat them."

      -Jason Day

28. "RELY ON MAKING A GOOD TURN WITH YOUR SHOULDERS," says Fred Couples.

Fred Couples is 5' 11", and weighs 185 lbs. He uses a TaylorMade SLDR 460 with a 9.5-degree loft.

"I'm not too concerned about moving my hips," Fred says. "I occasionally don't turn my shoulders to where my left shoulder is under my head."

"So, I usually concentrate on making a good shoulder turn."

He's also said, "I try to speed up and hit through the ball on my downswing."

Fred adds, "If I slow up on the downswing there's a better chance to miss hit or spin the ball."

Fred points out, "You don't want any excess spin as the ball could wind up anywhere if that should happen."

Fred gets good distance with a good shoulder turn.>
https://www.youtube.com/watch?v=mgdgwonPRIE

"I caddied for a guy who was a very good player, and he gave me a set of clubs, just a starter set: 5-iron, 7-iron, 9-iron, putter and driver. I just loved it."

"How I developed my swing was to just grab a club and start banging balls."

    -Fred Couples

29. "SEVEN SIMPLE WAYS TO GET YOUR BLOOD MOVING TO YOUR MUSCLES AND HIT IT LONGER"

You should always seek medical advice from your medical professional and/or check with your physician before doing the exercises and drills in this book or in any exercise program to avoid possible injury.

1. PRACTICE SWINGS.

Do 25 practice swings. Concentrate on tempo and balance.

2. SIMPLE STRETCH.

Stand or lie on the ground (if you can) and stretch your arms in all directions and (if you're lying down - extend your legs as long as you can - stretching both your arms and legs in every direction). Hold the stretch for 30 seconds and repeat 3 times.

3. BURPEES

Do 10 Burpees (without pushups). These will loosen you up and warm up your muscles.

4. ARM SWING

Simply swing your arms, up and down, side to side, in every direction for several minutes.

5. TURNING YOUR SHOULDERS.

Slightly bend your knees. Bend slightly forward. Let your arms hang down naturally. Swing your arms. Move your hips and legs while transferring your weight to the right and left.

6. SIMPLE JUMPING JACKS

Do 25 jumping jacks. This will get your heart pumping blood to your muscles.

7. TOE TOUCHES

Simply touch your toes pausing at the bottom for 10 seconds as you bend down and repeat 3 times.

"Training gives us an outlet for suppressed energies created by stress."

"It tones the spirit just as exercise conditions the body."

>	*-Arnold Schwarzenegger*

30. "BASIC STEPS IN DRIVING AND HOW TO GET YOUR GAME BACK" says Jordan Spieth

Driving the golf ball:

1. Justin recommends, "Tee the ball forward to catch the ball on the upswing to increase your angle of attack."

2. Also, "Before starting your down swing, turn your lead hip back before your upper body starts to turn."

3. "As you strike the ball, your weight should be on your left heel." He adds, "Stand up on your left heel straightening your left leg and pivot on your left leg."

4. "Keep in mind, your upper torso should be turning slower than your hips and your right shoulder should be lower than your left shoulder."

5. Finally, "Keep your head behind the ball." He adds, "Look at the back of the ball through your swing to keep your head stationary."

DRILL:

Hit a small bucket of balls using these five steps. And, as Justin recommends, "Reflect on what you want to accomplish before you hit range balls."

"If you are going to talk negative about a place, you're almost throwing yourself out to begin with because golf is a mental game."

-Jordan Spieth

Getting your game back:

When Dustin Johnson lost the 2015 US Open by missing a winning putt to win (and then missing a very short putt to put himself in a playoff which he could probably make blindfolded), he took a break and got away to Idaho.

Jordan, after losing the 2016 Masters with a quadruple bogey 7 on the 12th hole, took time off and went on a trip to the Bahamas with three other tour pros and simply relaxed and forgot about golf for a while.

"Laughter is an instant vacation."

-Milton Berle

31. LOUIS OOSTHOUSEN 500 YARD DRIVE.

April, 2013, Seoul, South Korea, The Ballantine's Championship.

Louis hit a drive off the tee onto a cart path on the right side of the hole and the drive didn't stop rolling for a minute and a half down the cart path for approximately 500 yards.

Here is Louis' drive >
https://www.youtube.com/watch?v=QXq-ZTPpRQ4

32. "PRACTICE HARD AND SOMETIMES YOU GET LUCKY," says Andrew McGee.

The 2001 Phoenix Open. Andrew tees off on the 17th hole, a 332-yard par 4. He scored an ace.

Andrew commented, "I just teed off with driver while Tom's was squatting on the green trying to line up his putt studying the line."

What was Andrew trying to do? "I was just trying to leave myself a shot 50 yards to the green."

"I didn't see it but my drive bounced on the green and glanced off Tom's putter he was holding by his side, and after glancing off his putter, the ball rolled into the hole 8 feet away."

Under the rules, it's a hole in one.

*

On March 26, 2015, Aaron Baddeley said after hitting a ball in the hole on the 347-yard par 4, 17th hole at the Texas Valero Open in San Antonio,

"I just thought I'd just hit it straight and so I hit it."

"I started walking and then heard the crowd going nuts, I was like, wait, I just made birdie."

Birdie?!

"I was hitting my third shot off the tee after hitting my first drive left and OB."

Aaron wound up shooting a 68 which left him one shot off the lead in the first round.

33. LONG DISTANCE AND ACCURACY? How to do it Sergio's way.

Sergio Garcia is 5 feet 10 inches tall, weighs 180 lbs., uses a TaylorMade M2 with 9.5-degree loft. He's also one of the most accurate in hitting fairways.

He recommends:

"Don't crouch over the ball but stand up tall and be relaxed and balanced."

Sergio adds, "Practice swinging to test your tempo and do a few practice swings making sure you're not swing too fast but with a nice even tempo."

Sergio adds, "When you stand more erect, you have more mobility in your swing."

"To do a more compact swing, I bring the club and both arms back in one piece bending my right elbow - keeping it close to my body."

Sergio adds, "I don't backswing all the way to bring the club parallel with the ground."

He has talked about his father. "My father taught me how to bring the club back on the downswing."

Expanding on this, "He told me to imagine I was pulling a chain down with both hands. Let the club lag behind your hands and whip the club through the ball."

He told me to, "Stay down through the shot."

Sergio advises how to keep your head down:

"Even though you've made impact with the ball, keep down and let your club and your arms finish. If you're hitting bad drives stay down longer on the ball."

"A way to check if you have the right tempo in your swing is to see if you still have balance after finishing the drive. If you're off balance, try swinging slower."

"When it comes to hitting solid drives, the secret is to swing within yourself."

"I know that sounds like a cliché, but it's true."

"If you swing at 100 miles per hour and hit it on the toe, you won't hit the ball as far as you would with an 80-mph swing that catches the ball in the center of the clubface."

-Sergio Garcia

34. FRANCESCO MOLINARI SAYS, "CHOOSE A SMALL TARGET."

Francesco Molinari averages over 297 yards and is also one of the most accurate drivers on Tour. He's 5' 8" tall, weighs 159 lbs. and uses a TaylorMade M1 2017 with an 8.5-degree loft.

He feels the most important thing to do before driving the ball is to find a small target.

"Some of the fairways are wide, and you don't hit without aiming at something. It's best to line up to a specific spot."

There an adage, "Aim small, miss small," says Francesco.

Francesco said, "After playing a hole with a tight fairway, players sometimes are relieved to come to the next hole with a wide-open fairway. Don't just hit it. Pick a precise target."

Keep a positive attitude. The game of golf can get the devil out of you:

"It's easy to see golf not as a game at all but as some whey-faced, nineteenth-century Presbyterian minister's fever dream of exorcism achieved through ritual and self-mortification."

-Bruce McCall

35. "YOUR DRIVER MAY BE STRAIGHTER THAN YOUR THREE WOOD UNDER THE LAWS OF PHYSICS FOR AMATEUR GOLFERS."

A three wood off the tee for amateurs doesn't always mean you've got a better chance to get it in the fairway.

The great Nancy Lopez played in many Wednesday Pro Ams and once said,

"Amateur golfers tend to swing harder off the tee with a three-wood trying to hit it as far as a driver."

She explains, "They want to hit great shots playing with a pro. You should just play your normal game. Don't add extra effort."

If you're playing a hole with a narrow fairway with deep rough on both sides, the added pressure in trying to get the ball on the fairway contributes to making a bad swing with the three wood or a long iron.

Under the laws of physics, the large head of the driver has a higher "Moment of Inertia" (i.e. a higher "angular mass" or "rotational inertia") than a three wood.

In other words, the larger club head of the driver is more stable.

The three wood has a smaller head. The path to the ball is not as stable as the driver.

Choke up on a driver instead of hitting a three wood. You will make better contact. Forget about missing and think positive like Michael Jordan who said,

"I've missed more than 9000 shots in my career."

"Twenty-six times I've been trusted to take the game winning shot and missed."

Golf Driving Techniques from Golfing Greats and Golf Stories

"I've failed over and over and over again in my life."

"And that is why I succeed."

    -Michael Jordan

36. "TEE THE BALL MY WAY," says Billy Horschel

Billy Horschel is 6' tall, weighs 175 lbs. He uses a PXG 0811X 9-degree Driver and averages 301.7 yards on his driving distance. A Univ. of Florida "Gator" and very popular on the Florida courses with fans.

Besides teeing up the ball half way up from the top edge of his driver, he also recommends, "Play the ball forward to increase the angle of attack with all of your weight lined up behind the ball."

When Billy needs a conservative drive to keep the ball in play on the fairway, "I hit my three wood and I know it will go about 265 yards."

He points out, "Swinging a three wood is closer to a swing with an iron or a five wood since you're trying to pinch the ball off the ground." And Billy adds,

"Less can go wrong that way compared to teeing up the ball."

37. BROOKS KOEPKA TIPS FOR A BIG DRIVE WHEN YOU NEED ONE.

Brooks Koepka is 6' tall, weighs 186 lbs. and uses a TaylorMade M2 with a 10.5-degree loft. He averages 309.3 yards driving the ball and it's his best stat which usually ranks him in the top ten on Tour. Brooks went to Florida State Univ. a "Seminole" and arch rivals of the Univ. of Florida "Gators."

His driving tips are:

1. "Flex and fix your feet into the ground. You don't want to slip."

"You can do this easier if you try to grip the ground with the bottoms of your shoes."

"It gives you a strong swing base."

Golf Driving Techniques from Golfing Greats and Golf Stories

2. Brooks points out, "Other players laughed at Tiger Woods for pulling out of the Farmers Insurance Open because he couldn't 'flex his glutes.'"

Brooks feels, "It's crucial to feel your right glute flex at the top of your swing."

"I do squats to keep in shape since your right glute is a power base as you begin your downswing."

3. "Turn your upper body as far to the right as you can since the faster you unwind, the faster you will create swing speed. Turn your back far enough so that it's facing your target."

4. Finally, "Build up your abs. Stronger abs mean faster turns with your upper body. Stronger abs also mean less pressure on your back."

38. "TO HIT IT BIG, SET UP CORRECTLY," says Adam Scott

Adam Scott 6 feet tall, 180 lbs. and uses a 9.5 degree Titleist 915D2.

"I hit it farther now because of my set up," says Adam who averages over 302 yards in driving distance.

He goes through set up steps:

1. "First, keeps your arms loose and hanging directly down from your upper body."

2. "Tilt your hips forward and stick your butt out and tilt your hips properly so your upper torso can coil more easily."

3. "The shaft of the driver should be pointed from the ground to your belt buckle. This tells me I'm the right distance from the ball."

4. "Keep your feet about shoulder width apart for good balance when you coil," he explains.

5. "Your neck should be in direct line with your spine and don't lift your chin."

6. "Your knees should be flexed slightly and you should feel comfortable and attached to the ground."

7. "Start your backswing with a one-piece takeaway with your arms and club moving back as one while beginning your turn."

8. At the top of the back swing, Adam doesn't think about turning his hips. "My swing thought is to turn my shoulders and my arms and the club will follow."

9. "Stay smooth and continue turning after hitting the ball and allow the club to carry your arms to the top of your swing."

39. "BIG DRIVING IS NOT WHAT YOU REALLY WANT," says Larry Mize.

Larry Mize is 6 feet tall, weighs 165 lbs. and won the 1987 Masters. He uses a Cleveland Launcher DST 8.5-degree driver.

He played the Tour from 1982 to 2001. He holds the record for having the shortest driving average on Tour of 244.9 yards.

There's an old saying, "There's no pictures on scorecards. So, hitting it big isn't a necessity."

Larry Mize won four times on tour including one Masters where he beat Greg Norman with a 150-foot chip in with a wedge. "I picked a spot and landed it right there." If he didn't chip in, Greg would have won easily.

40. "I JUST EXECUTE BASIC TECHNIQUES FOR A LONG DRIVE," says Tony Finau

Tony Finau is 6' 4" and weighs 200 lbs. He hits a Ping G LS Tec driver with a 9-degree loft. His drives average 306 yards.

He has a 124-mph swing speed and says his driving ability comes from just following the basic techniques.

"I'm feeling comfortable when I set up," says Tony. "I step forward with my right foot and place the driver head behind the ball to line up my shot."

Tony goes on to explain, "After I align the shot, I put my left foot in and balance my weight evenly."

He lets his arms hang down naturally to give him ease when swinging the club freely.

"I start my backswing by taking the club away smoothly in one piece and in one motion," Tony says. He adds, "I maintain the one-piece takeaway for as long as I can while turning my upper body."

He doesn't rush his backswing and starts his backswing with a turn of his left hip making sure he doesn't begin his down swing with his hands. Tony says, "If I start my downswing with my hands I won't hit it well."

When Tony plays in the Pro Ams on Wednesdays, he notices amateurs try to over hit and add speed by using their arms and hands more than they should. That actually slows the swing down.

Tony points out, "You have to let the speed build by itself and you can't force it." He tries to release the club as effortlessly as possible.

At the finish of his swing, he stands tall. Tony understands not everyone has his flexibility. So, he recommends you try to finish higher and with more balance and your drive will be further than you normally hit.

"It's better for amateurs to relax and play an even game in a pro-am." He adds, "The best shots come when you're relaxed and happy and your brain is telling the right muscles in your body to coordinate it all into a good golf shot."

"I've been a pro for almost eight years, and I'm starting to understand what it takes on tour."

"For starters, you can venture a little from who you are as a golfer, but don't mess with your swing DNA too much."

"Lee Trevino didn't become great by trying to hit high hooks, right?"

-Tony Finau

41. "WHAT MEN CAN LEARN FROM LADIES LONG DRIVING - WITH AN AVERAGE SWING SPEED OF 95 MPH."

The average male golfer has a swing speed of 95 mph. The LPGA ladies have an average swing speed of 95 mph.

According to most golf instructors, "The best women golfers in the world can't swing 120 mph like the men on the PGA Tour. Most swing at 95 mph like your average male golfer."

And, statistics show, "The best women golf drivers on the LPGA tour hit drivers average in the 260-yard range and there are some who average over 270 yards."

So most all instructors agree, "That women will generate more distance if they have an increased angle of attack." In general, "Women should use a wide stance, tee the ball farther ahead and drop their right shoulder."

"They keep their left arm extended out through the entire swing. Their wrists are naturally hinged at the top of their swing."

The natural swing for women is, "To bring the club back wide and once their left shoulder is under their left chin, they turn their left hip, knees, and upper torso letting the club come down as freely and effortlessly as possible keeping their head behind the ball and letting their wrists unhinge naturally as it strikes the ball."

"Women should image they are a pole and your arms are hanging down like two ropes," according to most instructors.

"Then when you swing a golf club, imagine you are in the process of wrapping the club around your body as you coil the club at the top of your swing."

Joanne Carner said, "The more you twist your upper body while keeping your left arm straight, the more you are coiling to whip the club at the ball and sweep it off the tee."

On the upswing, your weight has shifted to your right side. Joanne adds, "Your weight will shift to your left on the downswing during the process of sweeping the ball off the tee."

Finally, as Johnny Miller, the "Golden Boy", has said, "Open your hips to start your down swing and finish balanced keeping your left arm straight with most of your weight on the left side."

Johnny adds, "Your hips are the gas pedal to your swing."

"I build confidence when I practice a variety of shots - hitting it high or low, working the ball."

"A lot of golfers go to the range and just hit full shots."

"Full shots won't build on-course confidence, because you won't always hit full shots out there."

"My confidence is built on knowing I can effectively work the ball in any circumstance."

        -JoAnne "Big Mama" Carner

42. "TWO THINGS TO CURE A SLICE"

Many weekend golfers slice their drives.

Hank Haney advises, "A simple way to find the correct path is to draw the club away from behind the ball keeping it low to the ground."

Hank says, "Allow the bottom of the driver to slowly trace a path along the ground as you turn your body keeping your left arm straight with your head still and behind the ball."

"Don't try to swing hard," Hank says. "Swing smoothly instead to help you have your driver head square at impact."

Jason Dufner recommends, "Drop your right foot back to allow your body to turn easier."

"Take a wide takeaway and drop your right foot back so the toe is even with the heel of your left foot."

DRILL:

At the range hit a small bucket of balls dropping your right foot back and turn with a wide one piece takeaway with your club from the ball. Trace the bottom of the club along the ground as you bring the club back. Swing smoothly.

On the lighter side:

"It takes longer to learn to be a good golfer than it does to become a brain surgeon."

*"On the other hand, you don't get to ride around on a cart, drink beer, eat hot dogs and stare at the cart girl's t*ts all day if you are performing brain surgery."*

    -Anonymous

43. "THE TRANSITION FROM APEX TO STRIKING THE BALL."

Keegan Bradley is one of the longest hitters on tour. He's 6 foot 3 inches tall, weighs 190 lbs. and uses a TaylorMade M2 with a 10.5-degree loft. His drives average 300 yards.

The "Transition" is what you do when you bring the club down to strike the ball from the top of your swing.

"My first move of the Transition from upswing to downswing starts with turning my hips toward the target, says Keegan. He starts turning his hips slightly before he reaches the top of his swing.

"You have to have coordination and practice this. since it does create a lot of speed as your arms come down," says Keegan. However, most of us mortals cannot do this.

If you don't have the coordination, "A simple substitute to this is to start to transfer your weight to your left side at the top of your backswing by stepping on your left heel," says Keegan.

Keegan explains, "Your left knee will begin to slide back to its original position when you took your stance."

"This will create enough respectable club head speed to automatically hit the ball farther," says Keegan.

DRILL:

At the range, have the single objective of planting your left heel to begin your transition from the top of your swing.

As Keegan says, "Your left heel should be off the ground at the top of your swing and begin your downswing by simply stepping down on your left heel and let your arms follow."

Once you've feel you have this down, turn your single swing thought to turning your hips toward the target at the top of your swing and hit more range balls. Let your arms follow and keep your head behind the ball.

"You can't swing with hesitation; you can't try to steer the ball to the flag; you can't worry about that water hazard as you take the club back."

"You have to pick the right club, visualize the shot you want to hit, and then focus on that shot until the ball is gone."

-Keegan Bradley

44. "SOME SIMPLE POINTS TO REMEMBER"

Swinging hard will not make the ball go father.

"It's not about swinging hard, it's about other things totally different than swinging hard. Timing, coordination of hips and torso is what it's about," say many instructors."

They go on to say, "Your stance, and grip, and ball position are important and have no relation to swinging hard."

In summary, most of the pros say to "Tee the ball up higher and play the ball three to four inches from the level point on your down swing so you will be swinging up on it."

"Tee it high and swing normally. Catch the ball on the beginning of your upswing."

"If you want to hit it longer with your driver, the impact point with the driver should be where the club begins to ascend."

Golf Driving Techniques from Golfing Greats and Golf Stories

"So, get yourself accustomed to teeing up the ball forward and swinging wide and let it go!"

Golf Driving Techniques from Golfing Greats and Golf Stories

45. "JEFF BARDEL DRIVES IT 288 YARDS WITH ONLY ONE ARM."

Can you outdrive a guy with one arm?

Who hit the longest drive with only one arm. Jeff Bardel did it here > https://www.youtube.com/watch?v=INTwclOZudo

He didn't let the loss of an arm bother him. "I speak publicly on battling depression and increasing self-esteem and to inspire people, especially young people, to do the best with what you have."

*

Dr. Gary Wiren, a PGA Instructor, is 5 feet 11 inches tall and weighs 187 lbs. He's 75 years old.

Dr. Wiren said, "Getting older doesn't mean you can't hit it a long."

It's inevitable that as we age we lose strength and flexibility, but many golfers let it happen too soon."

Dr. Wiren not only "talks the talk" but also "talks the talk with his vigorous daily work outs.

His club head speed is 118 mph and can drive a ball over 300 yards.

Dr. Wiren says, "Golf courses are becoming longer and more difficult and are becoming less enjoyable for the weekend golfer."

"Golf courses should be made to be more fun and enjoyable for the average player." He is a staunch supporter and urges developers to make golf courses less difficult and more fun.

"Hitting a 300-yard drive is not unusual for young players."

"But it is unusual for a 75-year-old guy."

"I'm not saying you don't deteriorate with age. I'm saying most people deteriorate far too rapidly."

"You can actually get stronger and more flexible into your nineties, if you work at it…."

"As I lather up my face in the morning, I'll rise up on my toes to work my calves, or I'll tighten my glutes, my quads and my stomach."

"When I brush my teeth, I do 50 to 100 squats."

"When I pump gas, I put my leg up on a garbage can and stretch."

"What are you going to do — just stand there and watch the numbers go around?"

    -Dr. Gary Wiren

Golf Driving Techniques from Golfing Greats and Golf Stories

46. GET BACK TO BASICS.

In researching, reading and discussing how to drive a golf ball farther, we came across this very simple video showing the basics of driving a golf ball and taking the club away wide >
https://www.youtube.com/watch?v=8W89QnvY4Rg

"I've got a theory that if you give 100 percent all of the time, somehow things will work out in the end."

-Larry Bird

Golf Driving Techniques from Golfing Greats and Golf Stories

Thank you for taking an interest in our book. If you enjoyed it, please consider leaving a review on Amazon so more readers can find this title.

Golf Driving Techniques from Golfing Greats and Golf Stories

Team at Golfwell's Other Books

Absolutely Hilarious Adult Golf Joke Book

Golf Driving Techniques from Golfing Greats and Golf Stories

Team at Golfwell's Other Books

Fascinating Golf Stories and More Hilarious Adult Golf Jokes

Team at Golfwell's Other Books

Golf Putting Techniques from Golfing Greats and Sport Psychologists: Proven Putting Techniques from Tiger, Rory, Jason Day, Jordan Spieth, and Sports Psychologists

Team at Golfwell's Other Books

Why Do Little Fat Ladies Beat Me at Golf?
How to Correct Common Golf Mistakes

Golf Driving Techniques from Golfing Greats and Golf Stories

Team at Golfwell's Other Books

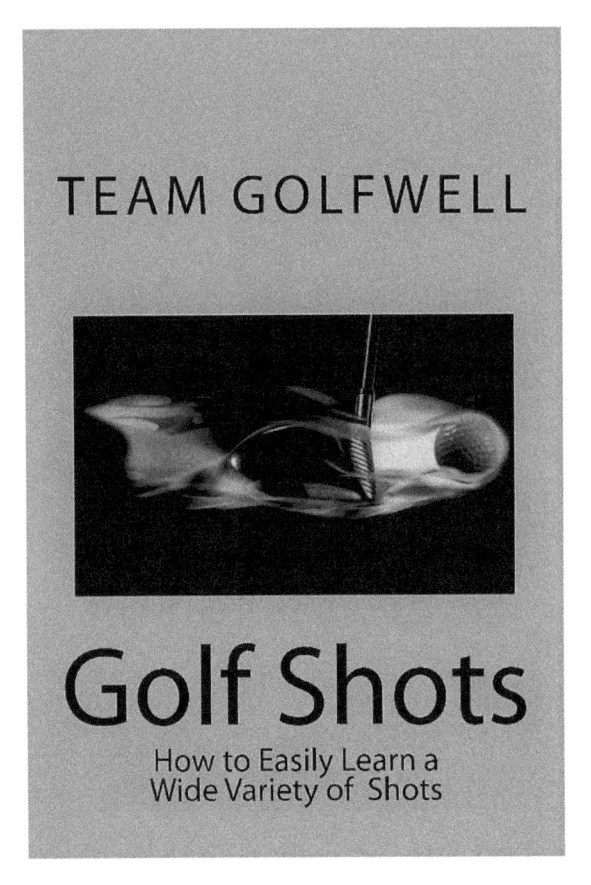

Golf Shots: How to Easily Learn a Wide Variety of Shots

Team at Golfwell's Other Books

Great Golf Formats: Betting Games, Adult Golf Jokes, and Stories

Team at Golfwell's Other Books

Walk the Winning Ways of Golf's Greatests: Golfing Greats Advice to Young Golfers

A final message to you from The Team at Golfwell:

Above all, have fun playing golf and enjoy all your adventures! Thank you for reading and best to you!

More about the Team at Golfwell

CPSIA information can be obtained
at www.ICGtesting.com
Printed in the USA
LVHW081614101219
640064LV00037B/1325/P